DON'T SAY NO, JUST LET GO

Don't Say No, Just Let Go

Living with Teenagers:
The Power Parenting Solution

by Maria Von Couver,

D.P.P., A.T.E., E.M.T., D.S.C.N.

PULP PRESS
Vancouver

To megan –
from the mother in
me to the mother in
you.
Maria Von
Couver
D.P.P. A.T.E.
etc etc

Published by
PULP PRESS BOOK PUBLISHERS
Arsenal Pulp Press Ltd.
100-1062 Homer Street
Vancouver, BC
Canada V6B 2W9

The Publisher acknowledges the ongoing assistance of The Canada Council and The Cultural Services Branch, British Columbia Ministry of Municipal Affairs, Recreation and Culture.

Cover: Kelly Brooks
Typesetting & Design: Vancouver Desktop Publishing Centre
Printing: Kromar Printing
Printed and bound in Canada

CANADIAN CATALOGUING IN PUBLICATION DATA:

Von Couver, Maria, 1948-
    Don't say no, just let go

    Includes index.
    ISBN 0-88978-242-3

1. Teenagers—Humour. 2. Child-rearing—Humour.
3. Parents and child—Humour. I. Title.
HQ796.V65 1991   649'.125   C91-091684-5

Table of Contents

PART THREE

Getting from where you are to where you wanted to be in the first place

List of Figures

DEDICATION

This book is dedicated to myself,
for I am the one who really
deserves it.

—MVC

Welcome to Power Parenting!

This book grew out of a series of revelations that began when my children became teenagers, and I found myself thinking I must have died and gone to hell. Only yesterday, it seemed, I was lying in hospital in my pink bed-jacket, cuddling a sweet little newborn and promising never to do all the terrible things to it that had been done to other children, including myself. But now, here I was running through the house after a sullen, monosyllabic, existentialism-sodden monster. I was waving a pair of scissors in the air and screaming, "Well then, I'll cut it for you!"

I knew then that I needed help.

Like many parents, I turned to the experts. (*Fact:* there are now 3.7 parenting experts per North American teenager.) I read their books, I went to their overpriced seminars, I cried in their offices. Worst of all, I tried to believe them when they described life with teens as a "challenge." My own experience told me that living with teens is not a "challenge"; living with teens is at best a bad dream and at worst a nightmare.

It began to dawn on me that my teens and I suffered most

when I tried to follow the experts' advice to *do the right thing*, and—in one way or another—*deal with* my teenagers. On the other hand, I noticed that whenever I found myself *not* dealing with my teens, a pleasant, peaceful atmosphere prevailed briefly in our home. I felt strong, confident, in charge of my life and my household.

So I asked myself, how can I consistently *not deal with* my teens? Well, the solution was right in front of me, in my adult relationships. I don't know about you, but I have plenty of grown friends and relatives who make perfectly ludicrous life decisions. When they announce these decisions, I don't say, "No." I don't say, "Over my dead body." I say, "Great, good idea, let me know how it turns out." What if I applied this supportive nonconfrontation to my life with my adolescent children?

At first, not dealing with my teens proved to be much harder than I had thought it would be. I had to force myself not to rise to the bait that was constantly dangled in front of me.

Teen #1: I flunked out of school and I'm not going back.

Me (through tears and clenched teeth): OK.

Gradually, my effort of will paid off. I was developing a benign, Zen-like nondecision to deal with them.

Teen #2: School sucks, man. I'm out of there.

Me: Hmm.

Eventually, I began to experience a distinct lack of interest in dealing with them.

Teen #3: School is a capitalist plot. I'm quitting.

Me: Great, good idea, let me know how it turns out.

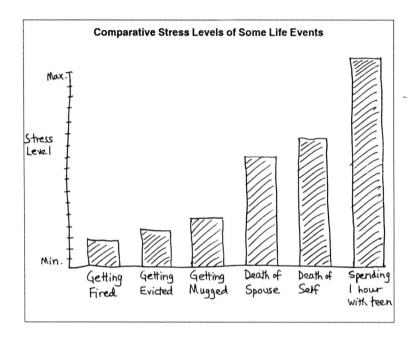

Comparative Stress Levels of Some Life Events

Stress Level (Min. to Max.):

- Getting Fired
- Getting Evicted
- Getting Mugged
- Death of Spouse
- Death of Self
- Spending 1 hour with teen

How liberating it was! My teens' new lifestyle enabled them to go ahead and do all the dumb stuff they were going to do anyway, and my new lifestyle enabled me to let go of my masochistic preoccupation with my teens and start writing down how I succeeded in not dealing with them.

Now I give these techniques to you—all the many creative ways of not dealing with teenagers that I have developed over the years. Together they are called the Power Parenting method, and their central philosophy is that there is only one way to get absolute power in your life with teens—Don't say no, just let go.

PART ONE

Toxic Teens, Poisoned Parents

CHAPTER ONE

The Toxic Teen

You can spend years striving to understand teenagers and the syndromes of teenage life. Sure, teens are easy to pity, surrounded as they are by Clearasil, boom cars, political causes and gang warfare. But take another look.

All around you, there are people in even deeper pain than teens: people who have yellow bags under their eyes, who cry themselves to sleep at night, whose hearts are swathed in scar tissue. No matter how much you study teens, these other people never go away. They are the victims of a devastating epidemic. They are the Poisoned Parents of Toxic Teens, and you may be one of them.

Do you suffer from Teen Toxicity?

Well, you're reading this book, aren't you? And there are hundreds of other physical and psychic symptoms, including but not limited to the yellow bags mentioned above.

If any of the following scenarios is familiar to you, you may well be the victim of a Toxic Teen:

✓ Your 13-year-old daughter told you she was staying at a friend's house overnight, and her friend told her mother she was staying at your place. Later you found out the two girls had been walking around downtown all night in their pink spandex short-shorts.

✓ You had your first date since you split up with your husband 7 years ago, and when you invited the date over for dinner, your son, 16, brought out all the old pictures of you and your husband in happier times.

✓ Your 17-year-old daughter took her entire share of a large family inheritance and bought a discarded, rusted-out, inoperative school bus with no windows or tires—from a "guy named Rick."

✓ When he goes out in public with you, your son wears a ski mask so that none of his friends will recognize him.

There is another dead giveaway: your sick tendency to cover up the emotional battering your teen has inflicted on you.

Example: Your 16-year-old son and his friends were caught driving through funeral ceremonies and mooning the mourners. You went on a two-week crying jag and finally sought help, saying it was something you ate.

Example: Your daughter, 14, went missing for two days, then phoned you to report that she had "caught a ride to Mexico" and needed you to wire her $200. By this time you had developed asthma, hives, rickets and hair loss. Incredibly, you told your doctor that your job was causing you a lot of stress.

And remember—the problem crosses all economic and ethnic lines. While the details vary from family to family, all Toxic Teens leave the same scars (the yellow bags, for example).

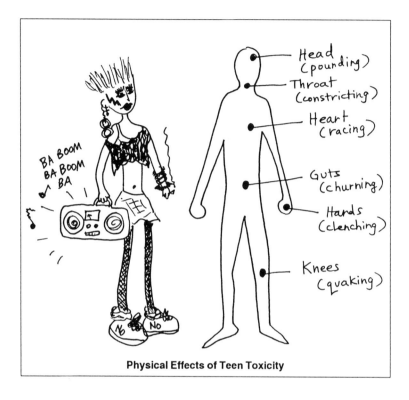

Physical Effects of Teen Toxicity

What causes Teen Toxicity?

There are experts who believe Toxic Teens are the product of over-permissive or over-repressive parents (parent-blaming is always in vogue with psycho-gurus, who have cushier jobs than parents). They will tell you that today's Toxic Teens are just yesterday's Toxic Tots—spitting puréed beet on freshly painted walls, secretly eating soap, unfurling rolls of toilet paper, etc. Another school holds that Teen Toxicity is probably *hormonal*, and therefore timeless. We've all seen those ancient cave-paintings in which adolescents turn up their noses at homemade clothing or enjoy a clandestine smoke behind a grove of pre-petrified trees.

Well, let the experts believe what they want to believe. All the theories in the world are no use to the Poisoned Parent.

Can you be detoxified?

The condition is rarely fatal, but it is debilitating. The nervous disorders will probably disappear when your teens leave home (see Chapter 11), but other effects, such as the yellow bags, may be permanent.

You live with teens, so you have already figured out that you can't change a Toxic Teen. *But you can change yourself.* You can become a Power Parent.

Early warning signs of Teen Toxicity

Four early signs of Teen Toxicity (verbal):

✓ "Everyone but me has a car."

✓ "I don't believe in birth control."

✓ "I can quit any time I want."

✓ "You can trust me."

Four early signs of Teen Toxicity (behavioural):

✓ Maintaining absolute silence for more than 90 days.

✓ Eating more than 3 lbs. or less than 3 oz. of food at any one meal.

✓ Sleeping with car parts.

✓ Being brought home by police officers.

CHAPTER TWO

The Five Parts of a Teen

The key to understanding your teen's bizarre behaviour—toxic one minute, fun and friendly the next minute—is to recognize that every adolescent has five separate yet interrelated parts.

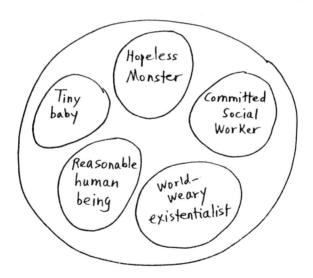

The Five Parts of a Teen

Emergence differential of the Five Parts

Any of the five parts of your teen may surface at any given moment.

> **Example:** Wilf has just turned 16. His room is such a pigsty he can hardly shut the door.

> *Tiny Baby:* Wilf refuses to clean his room, preferring to wallow in his own detritus as he did in the womb.

> *Committed Social Worker:* Wilf chides you for being hung up on one messy room when millions of children are hungry.

> *World-Weary Existentialist:* Wilf sighs, stares out at the rain and says that nothing matters, least of all the garbage festering in his room.

> *Hopeless Monster:* Wilf screams, slams doors, hurls profane accusations, and throws things when asked to return the eight coffee cups rotting in his room.

> *Reasonable Human Being:* Wilf cleans up his room because he can't find his favourite leather bracelet with the chromed iron studs.

> _____

> **Example:** Renee, 15, has been invited to a huge mid-winter party, the social event of the Grade Ten season.

> *Tiny Baby:* Renee argues strongly to stay out late at the party, and begs you with all of her body language to stop her from going.

> *Committed Social Worker:* Renee stays late at the party so she can organize her friends to attend the Anti-Everything rally next Friday.

World-Weary Existentialist: Renee goes to the party early and stays late, then comes home and pronounces it "dead boring, as usual."

Hopeless Monster: Renee screams, slams doors, hurls profane abuse, and throws things because she has "nothing to wear" to the party.

Reasonable Human Being: Renee stays home from the party because she has to get up early for work, and anyway "Skeeter" is out of town that weekend.

Shifting proportions of the Five Parts

At various stages in a teen's development, each of the five parts grows or shrinks in size. At age 14, the proportions look something like this:

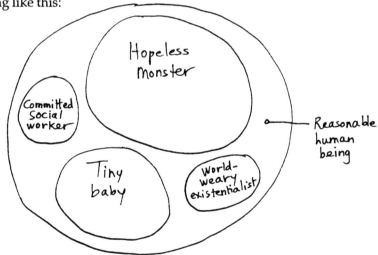

The Parts of a Teen (Age 14)

but by age 18, you should expect a considerable change.

The Parts of a Teen (Age 18)

Not every teen develops in the same way or at the same rate. It is normal for the components to change size randomly—every year, every day, every minute.

Accepting the Five Parts: The Whole Teen Approach

Recognizing and identifying the five parts of your teen is the first step to Power Parenting. The second step is to ignore all of the five parts equally. This is known, in modern parlance, as the Whole Teen Approach.

More important, the true Power Parent takes the Whole Parent Approach to herself. She does not have five parts. She has one part: the part that wants to live free of teen-induced anxiety and guilt.

FROM MARIA'S MAILBAG

Dear Maria:

My 18-year-old daughter has begun to advise me on make-up (I don't wear it) and fashion (I couldn't care less). She says, "Mom, you need Jojoba oil for those deep wrinkles around your eyes," and "This $20 peppermint foot oil should get the swelling down. I guess we can't do anything about the ankles." She has also plucked off all her eyebrows. Is she in the teen Committed Social Worker mode or is this really some kind of twisted Tiny Baby/Hopeless Monster revenge thing?
— *Confused*, Mozart, Sask.

Dear Confused:

Why bother to figure it out, when you could be tending your roses or writing letters to the Prime Minister, or whatever it is you like to do? Get a life.
— *Maria*

Dear Maria:

My wife and I separated last year and agreed on shared custody. Now our two teens play us off against each other. When they come to my apartment, they say, "At Mom's we don't have a curfew," and when they go there, they say, "At Dad's, we can drink as much beer as we want." I respect very much the work you've done around single parenting and double parenting, but what about that grey area in between, separated parenting?
—*Struggling*, Trois Rivières, Que.

Dear Struggling:

I recommend twist ties.
— *Maria*

CHAPTER THREE

Co-Teening
No More!

What is Co-Teening?

Co-teening is thinking, saying or doing anything that supports or encourages Toxic Teen behaviour. You are probably thinking to yourself, "No way would I do a fool thing like that!" But no parent co-teens on purpose. Indeed, most of them *don't even know they are doing it!*

Characteristics of a Co-Teen

✓ Desperately wants her teen to do normal things, such as speaking without mumbling and developing a taste for books that have words in them.

✓ Cannot stop herself from teen-referencing: her reality check is never herself, but the unconscionable thing her teen did yesterday, is doing right now or is certain to do tomorrow.

✓ Experiences constant doubt, fear and panic.

✓ Believes her teens' outrageous behaviour is somehow her own fault and wishes she had been a better parent, though she wonders how this would have been possible.

The bad news is that if you have any of these tendencies, you are probably a co-teen. The good news is that co-teening, like many other unforgivable acts, has now been identified as a sickness. Which means that you are no longer alone! And you can be healed.

FROM MARIA'S MAILBAG

Dear Maria:

I understand parents must get in touch with the Toxic Teen Within, but I think my wife is overdoing it. She bought us all 3-D glasses so we could watch a rock concert on cable TV, cooked Kraft dinner for supper every night last week, and used my car without permission. Our room is a complete mess and she hasn't had a haircut in months! When I confronted her, she said, "So?" and "Why are you always picking on me?" What should I do?

— *Anxious*, Edson, Alta.

Dear Anxious:

You have not yet grasped the essence of Power Parenting. *Let go,* even if it's your own wife. OK, she's gone overboard with the teen within stuff, but hey, she's feeling no pain. You, on the other hand, probably have eczema and palpitations. Relax, Anxious!

— *Maria*

The Co-Teening Disease Process

There are four levels of co-teening behaviour, ranging from the very subtle to the incredibly silly.

Level I Co-Teening: Bearing the cross

Example: Jillian, 13, has befriended a group of 17-year-old dropouts at the cappuccino bar. Father mopes around her, sighing heavily and looking burdened. She stays out later and later. Father goes grey and wrinkled. The school principal reports much cutting of classes. Father weeps silently into large snifters of brandy.

Level II Co-teening: Trying to fix it

Example: The Tremblay teens refuse to do any household chores. Mother and Father have become the Behaviour Mod Squad, offering the teens extra allowance to do the chores, withholding all allowance when they do not do the chores, offering gourmet dinners when they do the chores, withholding all dinners when they do not do the chores, offering late model sports cars when they do the chores, etc.

Level III Co-Teening: Covering up

Example: Chantelle has recently turned 14. When she smokes cigars in front of Father's business associates, he tells them she is rehearsing for a school play. When she gets her head shaved and shows up during Father's party, he tells his friends she is having chemotherapy. When she engages his bridge club in conversation filled with s--- and f---, he tells them she is a tragic victim of Tourette's Syndrome.

A Typical Co-Teening Genogram

 Mother of teens

 Toxic teen

 Father of teens

 Toxic teen's best friend, also son of father's boss

 Dormant toxic teen

 Young child

 Young child's good pal, who emulates toxic teen

 Mother of good pal, whom young child likes better than real mother, and whom toxic teen once saw nude.

 Father's boss, once married to cousin of young child's good pal's mother.

 Maternal grandfather of toxic teen, who loves dormant toxic teen best and suspects young child's good pal is his son.

Level IV Co-Teening: Out-teening the teen

Example: Bruce, 16, has fallen in with a motorcycle gang. Before long, Mother finds herself wearing skin-tight black leather garments, flipping the high sign to filthy men on Harley Davidsons, and craving Jack Daniels for breakfast.

In all of these cases, the parent's life centres on the Toxic Teen. Therefore the teens have no choice but to remain toxic, or what purpose in life do their parents have?

The Co-Teening healing process

Confronting the Toxic Teen Within

You were once a teen yourself, and you went to astonishing lengths to torment your parents. Remember? Get in touch with the Toxic Teen who still lurks in your psyche. Then you can take that first important step to joyful recovery.

Letting the teen within do without

Everyone has a Toxic Teen inside, but only the Power Parent gives that teen its voice, then ignores everything it says. Don't say no, just let go.

Healing the Battered Parent Within

Let's go back to our examples and offer those besieged families some Power Parenting solutions:

✓ Jillian's father has got to get a lover, or at least a personal computer.

✓ Mother and Father Tremblay should take up oil

painting or lawn mower racing, then everyone in the family can relax.

✓ Why does Father keep inviting people over?

✓ As for Bruce's mother, let her experience remind us that there is a world of difference between "don't say no" and "me too."

CHAPTER FOUR

A Professional Dialogue

Recently I attended an international symposium on teen parenting. One controversial panel discussion was on Duplex Families: the Effect on Unrelated Teens of Their Single Parents Moving In Together. On the panel were my colleagues, Drs. Von Chan, Von Diego, Von Geist, and Von Sidhu, as well as myself. So that you might understand what Power Parents are up against at the "expert" level, here is an excerpt of that session.

> *Von Diego:* I must posit that the transformational boundaries of the Duplex Family have serious phenomenological repercussions.

> *Von Chan:* But within the interstices of a societal expectation, which still has a socio-evolutionary memory of the extended family, the resolution is not a true paradigm shift.

> *Von Couver:* Either way, they're going to be a pain in the neck until they're at least 19 years old.

The Seminar Table

1. Von Sidhu; 2. Von Geist; 3. Von Chan; 4. Von Couver; 5. Von Diego

Von Geist: There is an implication of a comprehension of the formation of adolescent psycho-intellectual evolution that transcends the relational confines of—

Von Sidhu: No, no! Forgive me for interrupting, Doctor, but there has been no instigation of a transposition of the Duplex Causality Curve, crucial to any discussion of subjugation or liberation.

Von Couver: Is anyone doing research on freeze-drying teens and thawing them out later, after we figure out what to do?

Von Diego: Interrelational stress tendencies may be interdeterminantly comparable, in the hegemony of the relational sphere.

Von Couver: Yes, teenagers all over the world are impossible to live with.

31

Von Geist: Let me sum up, learned colleagues, with the proposition that the situational parameters of the Duplex Family impact substantially on dialogic signals in the parental inflow-outflow diametric.

Von Couver: In other words, don't say no, just let go.

Von Sidhu: Hear! Hear!

FROM MARIA'S MAILBAG

Dear Maria:

Every time I come home from the grocery store, my twin teenaged daughters make a terrible fuss about the plastic bags, the laundry detergent and the bleached toilet paper. They refuse to eat any cookies made by companies that invest in South Africa. They stomp on American products to protest Free Trade. I would appreciate your advice.
— *Victimized*, Gimli, Man.

Dear Victimized:

Rarely do I advise embryonic Power Parents to out-teen their teens, but in this case I must make the exception that proves the rule. You must begin shopping only at politically correct health food stores and co-ops. Within 14 days your teens will be so sick of sawdust breakfast cereal, fruit juice made by local but incompetent manufacturers, and unhomogenized milk swarming with gelatinous fat globules—all brought home in those cloth carry-bags that mush everything together and smell bad—that they will beg you to return to the old ways.
—*Maria*

PART TWO

Empowering the Power Parent

CHAPTER FIVE

Learning to Let Go: *just say "Good for you"*

Four responses that never work

- ✓ "Over my dead body."
- ✓ "Save it for marriage."
- ✓ "When I was your age . . ."
- ✓ "I don't care what everyone else's mother lets them do."

Responsophobia:
The fear of getting it wrong

Think back to the last time your teen said or did anything that shocked, surprised, disgusted and/or wounded you. Now try to recall what you were thinking one hour later:

- ✓ I was too lenient.

✓ I was too strict.

✓ I was too political.

✓ I was not political enough.

✓ I gave her too much responsibility.

✓ I was too protective.

If you thought any of these things, you have *responsophobia*, the completely rational fear of reacting at all to your teen.

Now, the Power Parent would *not think any of these things*. The Power Parent has only one response to everything her teen says or does: "Good for you." Yes, that's all there is to it!

Getting to Good for You

OK, it isn't as easy as it sounds. But after a few weeks of practice, you'll find that not only are you saying "Good for you," *you are believing it!* You will experience feelings of freedom that will not be matched until your teens leave home.

> **Example:** Your daughter, age 13, has found her first boyfriend. She says he is kind, smart, cute and likable. When you ask how old he is, she says he just turned 24. You say:
>
> WRONG: He's old enough to date me.
> RIGHT: Good for you.

> **Example:** Your son's voice cracked during his solo in the gala spring concert, so now he's been in his bedroom for 10 days and refuses to come out. You say:
>
> WRONG: Come out here, you little wimp.
> RIGHT: Good for you.

Example: Your daughter withdrew her savings from the bank and blew all of the money on video games in 20 minutes. You say:

WRONG: Why didn't you just flush it down the toilet?

RIGHT: Good for you.

Example: Your 16-year-old son wears battle fatigues, shaves his head, subscribes to reactionary magazines and accuses you of living before he was born. You say:

WRONG: You are a fascist running dog of the imperialist military-industrial complex.

RIGHT: Good for you.

FROM MARIA'S MAILBAG

Dear Maria:

A few days ago I noticed a peculiar odour emanating from my 14-year-old daughter's bedroom. I tried to let go, but today the smell was so foul I could not stop myself from entering her room. Imagine my surprise when I discovered two teenagers I had never seen before. They told me their parents didn't understand them and that my daughter had said they could live with us. Help!
— *Frantic*, Nepean, Ont.

Dear Frantic:

Power Parenting is about trusting your own negligence. How long do you think your daughter will be happy in that room with two trapped adolescents? You don't have to do everything, you know. And by the way, what was that bad smell?
— *Maria*

Example: Your son has joined a rock band called Pond Scum, which performs in clubs you are too old to get into, and has an act involving live banana slugs and rock salt. You say:

WRONG: Why can't you join Junior Achievers, like your cousin Ralphie?

RIGHT: Good for you.

Example: Your daughter tells you she is moving out on the weekend to join the Rainbeaux, quasi-religious nomads who wear grey and drive up and down the west coast worshipping rain clouds. You say:

WRONG: Why be born again?—surely once was enough.

RIGHT: Good for you.

Example: Your son's outfit for a visit to your extremely conservative parents: a leather jacket spray-painted with the words "Death Lust," torn blue jeans that reveal areas of his jockey shorts, and buttons that read "So What," "Who Cares," and "Up Yours." You say:

WRONG: I certainly hope your grandpa's papers are in order.

RIGHT: Good for you.

Example: Your daughter has become the Vegan Without a Cause. She refuses to eat at the table when animal products are served and she leaves provocative anti-vivisectionist literature on your pillow. You say:

WRONG: People who live on French fries eventually go blind.

RIGHT: Good for you.

Example: Your daughter is on her way out to meet a boy she found on the Parti-Wires, a public service that introduces strangers on the telephone. You say:

WRONG: Why don't you just get a T-shirt that says VICTIM on it?

RIGHT: Good for you.

Getting to Good for Me

When you learn Good for You, the big bonus is Good for Me. That is, Good For You transfers the burden of responsibility for your teens to the teens themselves, and you are free of it. The hours you used to spend crying, worrying and leaving messages on your doctor's answering machine, you can now spend playing golf, reading murder mysteries, going to Chant for Monetary Success workshops—whatever *you* like to do.

When you say Good for You, believe it. Let yourself become absolutely self-centred. Let yourself be a Power Parent.

FROM MARIA'S MAILBAG

Dear Maria:

My 15-year-old daughter got her high school annual signed by a number of chums who addressed her as "Ellie, you slut," "Dear Ellie, or should I say Blaze Starr," etc. Are these just teen jokes, or . . . ?

— *Aggrieved*, Weyburn, Sask.

Dear Aggrieved,

Don't tell me you haven't any reading material more stimulating than a high school (yawn) annual!

— *Maria*

Dear Maria:

Last night my husband and I came home early from Bridge Club to find our 16-year-old son wearing my best dress! My husband said it looked better on him than it did on me. What do you think of that?

— *Furious*, Qidi Vidi, Nfld.

Dear Furious:

If that's what your husband thinks of that dress, why not give it to your son? Let go, Furious!

—*Maria*

CHAPTER SIX

Parent Throttling

Pre-Power Parents labour under twin illusions:

✓ it is possible to reason with teens about their feelings

✓ it is desirable to reason with teens about their feelings

"Reason" and "feelings" simply do not belong in the same sentence. Asking a hormone-crazed teen or a guilt-crazed parent to make sense of her feelings is like teaching a dog to read a book—it only brings humiliation upon both of you. Besides, when the experts say "reason with," they really mean "manipulate," which never works. Teens learn so fast that minutes after you begin "reasoning with" them, you'll be left in the dust, manipulationally speaking.

> **Example:** Bonnie, 16, has planned a glorious weekend. Friday after school she and her best friend will hang out at the mall. They will then go to the Bijou with their boyfriends to see "Spread-Eagle Chicks: The Movie." All four teens will spend the night at Bonnie's friend's house (the friend's mother is out of town). On Saturday afternoon Bonnie will come home, shower and dress in an outfit that includes Mother's suede boots. She will

then go to a big party on the other side of town and take the last bus home, alone, at 1:00 a.m. On Sunday she will sleep all morning, sunbathe all afternoon, eat dinner and do a bit of homework.

In the old days, the communication process unfolded like this:

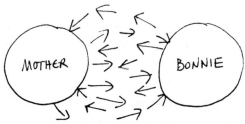

MOTHER: You WHAT? And WHAT? WHERE? (etc.)

BONNIE: You never want me to have any fun.

MOTHER: You and I have a contract about your household chores.

BONNIE: I have to do everything around here.

MOTHER: You and I have talked about misogynist pornography, haven't we, Bonnie?

BONNIE: You don't own me.

MOTHER: And don't I have a right to wear my suede boots on Saturday night?

BONNIE: Go ahead, ruin my outfit, I'll just wear something ugly.

Effective Parent Throttling (EPT)

Bonnie, a child of the 1970s, soon learns to decode Mother's feelings and make "I-statements" rather than "You-statements":

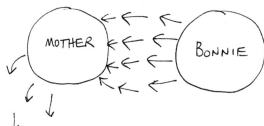

MOTHER: You WHAT? And WHAT? WHERE? (etc.)

BONNIE: I hear you being upset about many of my plans. Can we sort out your issues?

MOTHER: Um, my what?

BONNIE: I feel you are uncomfortable about me going to the Bijou and not doing any housework.

MOTHER: Well, yes . . .

BONNIE: I imagine you are jealous that I look about 300% better in your suede boots than you do. You worry that I'll get pregnant or get a dose or a bad reputation if I sleep with my boyfriend.

MOTHER: Yes, all of that. But I want you to have fun.

BONNIE: Great! See you later, Mom.

The EPT dynamic allows Bonnie to be a Toxic Teen wrapped in the clothing of a mature, understanding person.

Affirmative Dynamic Effective Parent Throttling (ADEPT)

Similar to the EPT dynamic but even more insidious is ADEPT, in which Bonnie uses affirmation-like language to disable Mother's rage-anxiety matrix.

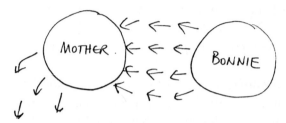

↓ MOTHER: You WHAT? And WHAT? WHERE? (etc.)

BONNIE: I feel you are very worried and angry.

MOTHER: Of course I am.

BONNIE: It makes me feel so secure to have such a concerned mother!

MOTHER: (crying) Please don't stay overnight with your boyfriend.

BONNIE: That's great, Mom! Let it out!

Integrated Non-exclusive Effective Parent Throttling (INEPT)

Once they have fallen for EPT and ADEPT a few times, even pre-Power Parents are quick to move to INEPT:

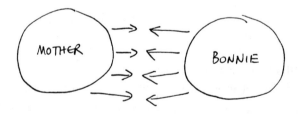

MOTHER: I know you're really looking forward to this weekend.

BONNIE: I feel you are very anxious about my plans.

MOTHER: I am very uncomfortable with some of the plans.

BONNIE: I am very uncomfortable with your discomfort.

MOTHER: The weekend you have planned just won't work for
me.

BONNIE: The weekend you have planned just won't work for
me.

Mother and Bonnie are locked in cross-manipulation for the
rest of their lives, and they don't even get the satisfaction of
hurling vicious insults at each other as they would in the old
days.

Power Ratio Establishment for Counteracting
Effective Parent Throttling (PRECEPT)

PRECEPT is the healthy Power-Parenting alternative to EPT,
ADEPT, INEPT and all the other EPTs of the pesky me-first era.
PRECEPT works, because Power Parenting is not a matter of
trickery or pseudo-democracy. It is a matter of letting go.

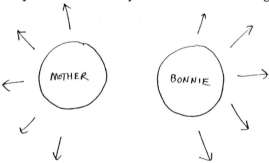

MOTHER: Good for you.

If PRECEPT seems scary, go deeper into your fears. What is
the worst thing that can happen? Bonnie might be exposed to
pornography, ruin Mother's suede boots, have sex with her
boyfriend, and fail to do household chores for three days. All of
this is going to happen anyway, if not this weekend, then some
other weekend. Mother refuses to take it on, redirecting her
energy to her own needs. She is calm and confident. She is a
Power Parent.

CHAPTER SEVEN

Teensactional Analysis

Let's look at it another way. Every exchange between ME (the parent) and YOU (the teen) is called a teensaction, and every teensaction is loaded—even thoughtless, innocent small talk. Over the years, the teensactions build into dynamics, most of them hopelessly sick.

> **Example:** 15-year-old Marla wants to get a tattoo on her belly, a sprawling hearts-and-snakes extravaganza that features largely the name of her new boyfriend. What does Mother say?

1. Good for Me, Bad for You

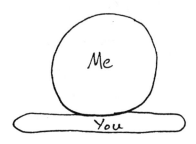

Mother contacts every tattoo parlour in a 50-mile radius and threatens to fire-bomb them if they touch her daughter. She launches a lawsuit against Marla's boyfriend, who, she is sure, dreamed up this preposterous plan. She reminds Marla that as long as she is under age 19, she can still be signed over to reform school.

2. Bad for Me, Good for You

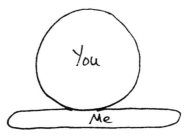

Mother lets Marla get her tattoo. In fact, she lends her the money to do it. Marla thinks Mother is the greatest. Mother knows that she has the backbone of a common garden slug. She also knows that although life is peaceful now, in six months Marla will turn on her, saying, "How could you let me disfigure my body with the name of that major loser!"

3. Bad for Me, Bad for You

I admit here and now that I did not invent Power Parenting, I merely reclaimed the concept. The Power Parent has been with us since the beginning of time.

Ancient Moms

Also known as Metaphysical Moms, these parents sent their young adults off to the circus all day while they gathered in the city-states, learning how to think and how to write poetry.

Moms in the Middle Ages

Medieval Moms never worried about their teens, preferring to maintain a simple loving faith that everything would turn out all right. Privately they were thankful for the fall of Rome, which had been a bad influence on their adolescent children.

Renaissance Moms

Those who were not burned as witches declined to fuss about curfews and haircuts, as everyone was far too busy inventing the printing press and the landscaped garden.

Reformation Moms

What with the Inquisition, the Counter Reformation, and creeping Calvinism, no one had time for acne or alienation.

Through the Ages

Enlightenment Moms

The long tradition of Power Parenting began to falter with the emergence of Enlightenment Moms (not to be confused with modern Enlightened Moms, who falter so often they can hardly stand up). But then, anxiety about teenagers was bound to crop up in an age that favoured reason, philosophy and conversation.

Industrial Moms

Snatching Power Parenting from the jaws of defeat, Industrial Moms put their teens to work in factories and sweatshops, leaving no question about who was in charge here.

Modern Moms

From the Roaring Moms of the '20s, the Depressive Moms of the '30s, and the Patriot Moms of the '40s, came the Beatnik and Storybook Moms of the '50s and '60s. Postwar wealth made possible the phenomenon of the rec room, placing teens out of sight and, consequently, out of mind.

Postmodern Moms

'70s Hippie Moms wanted their teens to be free, if they knew which ones were theirs in the first place. Hippie Moms set the stage for '80s Punk Moms, who shocked the world by drying baby diapers for re-use (without washing them first) and out-teening their teens by sticking safety pins through their own noses and ears.

Power Parents

Making the empowerment choice in the face of relentless "expert" behaviour-mod advice, these are the bravest parents in history, and a shining example for the parents of the future.

Mother accuses Marla of having sex with her boyfriend. Marla says, "If you can have sex with your boyfriend, I can have sex with mine." Mother reminds Marla that she was rude to her boyfriend the last time he came over. Marla says she learned rudeness by listening to Mother talk to her. Mother says Marla learned rudeness from that slut Angela she hangs out with, the one who made Marla's grades go from As to Cs in one semester. And so on.

4. Good for Me, Good for You

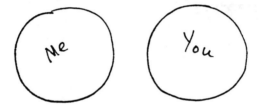

Mother can only hear part of what Marla tells her, because she's in a luxurious bubble bath, running the hot water. "Great, honey," she shouts at the door. "I'm glad you're over your phobia about needles. Pick up a head of lettuce on the way home, will you?"

CHAPTER EIGHT

Communicating with Teens: *A contradiction in terms?*

The proof is in the mind-mapping

By now you are ready to face facts. When either teen or parent says, "I hear where you're coming from," she is lying. You can prove this for yourself in a mind-mapping ("clustering") session with your own teen. Bribe her if you must to go through it with you. You choose a word or idea, then each of you charts her random musings on that word or idea.

Following is an actual example of a mind-mapping session. Parent and teen chose the word MONEY, then went into separate rooms and "clustered" independently for 10 minutes. The two resulting mind-maps:

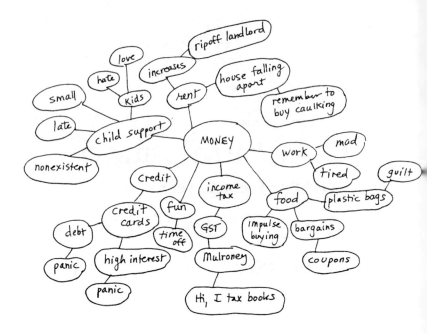

The Parent Mind-Map

Look carefully at these mind-maps.

✓ The money-food path for the parent is MONEY →
FOOD → PLASTIC BAGS → GUILT, while the
money-food path for the teen is MONEY → SPEND
→ RESTAURANTS.

✓ The teen mind-map displays no concern at all with
such urgent money issues as HIGH INTEREST,
CHILD SUPPORT, COUPONS or REMEMBER TO
BUY CAULKING.

✓ Although both mind-maps display a loathing for
paid employment, the parent mind-map path is
MONEY → WORK → TIRED or MONEY → WORK
→ MAD, whereas the teen path is a breezy MONEY
→ JOB → HATE → QUIT.

The Teen Mind-Map

✓ The only money-related destination parent and teen
have in common is FUN. But for the parent, FUN
connects with TIME OFF, while for the teen, FUN is
associated with SNOW-BOARDING.

Why parents and teenagers cannot talk

We all know parents of teenagers who make frequent and
pathetic attempts to "keep the lines of communication open."
To teens, this expression has to do with paying the monthly
phone bill.

The fact is, words and expressions you take for granted have
very different meanings for teens.

Word	Teen Definition	Parent Definition
Grad	Fun-party-freedom	Drink-puke-screw
Sex	Fun-hot-forbidden	Exploitation-pregnancy-AIDS
Drugs	Fun-high-party	Sick-freakout-cops
Cars	Fun-fast-power	Crash-blood-cops
Sibling	Brat-swear-fight	Fun-secrets-support
Friend	Fun-secrets-support	Bad influence

Some words have even more complex meanings.

Sample Word: *Conversation*

Teen Boy	Teen Girl	Parent
Two guys grunting and cursing side by side at a hockey rink.	Three or more girls all talking at once.	Teen states opinion, parent corrects it.

Sample Word: *Power*

Teen Boy	Teen Girl	Parent
Talking the most and loudest or driving the most and loudest or spending the most and loudest	Having the oldest boyfriend	Having the most trouble-free teens

Sample Word: *Great movie*

Teen Boy	Teen Girl	Parent
Full Metal Jacket	*Heathers*	*The Big Chill*

When talking is absolutely necessary

Long periods of silence between parent and teen can be very positive. They have a healing effect because they eliminate the need for excessive worry. No news is good news, right?

However, there will be times when you simply *must* talk to your teen, and vice versa. What can you do?

Four approaches to talking that always fail:

- ✓ "How was school today?"
- ✓ "Let's share our feelings."
- ✓ "How was the party last night?"
- ✓ "You never talk to me."

Four approaches to talking that always succeed:

- ✓ "Don't you think it's about time you quit school?"
- ✓ "Here's $200, spend it on anything you want."
- ✓ "Got any hash?"
- ✓ "I have sold your baby sister."

The idea here is to get the conversational ball rolling by getting your teen's attention. Then all you need are the following easy techniques for getting through the actual talking period.

Non-adjudicational monitoring

Incline your head toward your teen. Purse your lips and furrow your brow as though deeply pondering her words. Nod understandingly from time to time.

Example: Judith has just come home from the movies and she needs to talk about it.

1. The pre-Power Parent conversation:

JUDITH: OK so like there was this tall blonde, right, and—

MOTHER: Tall blond *woman*, Judith.

JUDITH: And she has this boyfriend and he like really loves her, right, but then she like gets in this accident, right?

MOTHER: Stop saying "like" and "right" all the time!

JUDITH: OK, so like—I mean—OK so she, oh yeah but before that, I forgot, she like—oops, OK there was this other guy—

MOTHER: (yawning) Well, honey, it's past my bedtime.

JUDITH: OK, just forget it, you bag!

2. The Power Parent conversation:

JUDITH: OK so like the other guy, the first one, like he was rilly nice, right, but the blonde, like she only thought this other guy, Dave, no—Ron I think it was, like that he was the rilly rad one eh, only—no it wasn't Ron it was Dave, or was it Ron, OK so anyway but *before* the thing about the legs, eh? You know what I mean?

MOTHER: Mm-hmm.

Non-lingual messaging interpretation

Decoding the unspoken language of adolescents is one of the great unsung arts. Start with these common examples, then build your own glossary.

What Your Teen Does	What Your Teen is Saying
Rolls eyes	Does she have to wear that gross sweater all the time?
Glances at watch	I'm missing *fifteensomething*.
Crosses and uncrosses legs	I wonder if my thighs look too fat when I do this.
Winces	I can't believe he still says "groovy."
Yawns	Sure hope I get a Nintendo for my birthday.
Refuses to eat breakfast	No way can I sit at a table with my family for ten whole minutes.

Caution: Sometimes the non-lingual messaging signal is not a cover-up:

What Your Teen Does	What Your Teen is Saying
Rolls eyes	This mascara is too thick.
Glances at watch	I wonder what time it is?
Crosses and uncrosses legs	I have to go to the bathroom.
Winces	Growing pains again.
Yawns	I'm tired.
Refuses to eat breakfast	I'm not hungry.

Storying

Storying means telling your teens anecdotes from your own adolescence. Sound silly? Not when you consider how your own teen years are portrayed in pop culture. Has anyone your age actually ever seen a beatnik wearing a beret and a pointy little beard, snapping his fingers and calling people "Daddy-O"? This is what our teens think we were like! No wonder they don't want to share their feelings with us.

So don't be shy. Tell them how you ran away from home at age 16 and lived for 3 months in your boyfriend's car before being caught. Or the time your parents went away for the weekend and you accidentally burned the house down. Or how you met your teens' father: a pay phone was ringing, you picked it up, and the rest is history.

Avoid glamorizing these memoirs. Tell your teen how hard it is to bathe in a Chevrolet, how sad you were about the guitar you lost in the fire, what it was like to find out that you can get pregnant on a pay phone.

Teen Curfew Egg Chart

**You don't have to break an egg if
you aren't going to make an omelette.**

  Your teen breaks curfew once
every 6 months.

  Your teen breaks curfew once
every month.

 Your teen breaks curfew once
every day.

  Your teen does not have a curfew.

FROM MARIA'S MAILBAG

Dear Maria:

Is it OK to smoke pot with my teenagers?
— *Perplexed*, Kapuskasing, Ont.

Dear Perplexed:

Only if it's their pot.
— *Maria*

Dear Maria:

Recently my son came home from school and reported that they'd had sex education in his guidance class. The teacher was very open about everything, which was fine with me up to the part where he ate a handful of Delfen foam, "to prove it doesn't taste bad." What should I do?
— *Distraught*, 100 Mile House, B.C.

Dear Distraught:

Get that man's name and phone number and send it to me at once.
—*Maria*

CHAPTER NINE

Teen Health

When little kids are sick, they're sick. Alas, the ailments of teens are not so uncomplicated. Many an unwary parent has been drawn into a vortex of confusion, pity and suspicion when her teen is indisposed. This guide will save you hours of distress as you deal with teen maladies over the years. And remember, the guide is not meant as medical advice. When in doubt, call your family physician, if she is not avoiding you.

Common teen symptoms and treatment

Symptom	Probable diagnosis	Treatment
Aural hypo-sensitivity (deafness)	Heavy metal music played on powerful Walkman	Stop talking to teen, she can't hear you anyway
Aural hyper-sensitivity (ability to hear any noise from long distances)	Really juicy argument going on in home	Postpone fight until teen goes out
Nausea	Recent overindulgence in pizza and/or beer	Ignore teen

Bloodshot eyes	Recent overindulgence in violent Hollywood cop shows	Learn psychic numbing
Itchy scalp	Cheap hair dye *or* Under-bathing *or* Over-bathing *or* Head lice	Build private residence for teen
Other maladies	Various	Mind own business

Conditions that often require medical attention	Conditions that often do not require medical attention
Acne	Acne
Coughing	Coughing
Twitching	Twitching
Bleeding	Bleeding
Bones protruding from torn flesh	Bones protruding from torn flesh
Rashes	Rashes
Screaming in pain	Screaming in pain
Unconsciousness	Unconsciousness

Teen maladies that can be treated

The Power Parent recognizes the difference between injury/illness (see above), which is usually best treated with active neglect, and grotesque symptoms described by teens, but invisible to anyone else:

Overbite	Body too angular
Underbite	Breasts too small
Chin too pointy	Breasts too large
Chin too round	Penis too small
Eyebrows too bushy	Wrong shape bum
Eyebrows too sparse	Wrong colour eyes
Nose too large	Voice too high

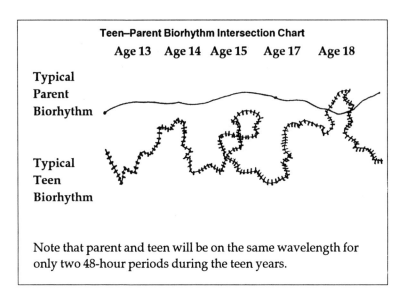

Teen–Parent Biorhythm Intersection Chart

Age 13   Age 14   Age 15   Age 17   Age 18

Typical
Parent
Biorhythm

Typical
Teen
Biorhythm

Note that parent and teen will be on the same wavelength for only two 48-hour periods during the teen years.

Nose too small	Voice too deep
Adam's apple too big	Wrong shape fingernails
Teeth crooked	Wrong shape feet
Bowlegged	Too much body hair
Knock-kneed	Not enough body hair
Early menstruation	Lips too thin
Late menstruation	Lips too full
Body too short	Knees too bony
Body too tall	Knees too fleshy
Body too round	Wrong colour hair
Wrong shape thighs	Feelings too sad

Two simple home remedies are always effective for the complaints listed above: Belgian chocolate and cash.

CHAPTER TEN

Timeless Paths of Power Parenting

All animals know how to parent. It is the most natural biological function in the universe. This is true and, in its way, beautiful. But remember: animals do not have teenagers. People do.

The New Age movement, with its blend of parapsychology, Eastern mysticism and capitalist fundamentalism, is a wonderful source of Power Parent techniques. The New Age guides the Power Parent to her rightful place in the universe—dead centre.

Chanting for power

The Power Parent strives for a tranquil, positive state of mind. Borrow liberally from Eastern-style meditation and get yourself a mantra—a word, phrase, or prayer that you repeat many times while relaxing physically.

> **Example:** Your daughter drove your car into the tree behind the garage.

Example: Your son was arrested for shoplifting at a department store full of warning signs, closed-circuit cameras, and obvious plainclothes detectives.

Pull the shades, remove your shoes, lie down, close your eyes and say these words over and over and over again: Good for Me, Good for You. Good for Me, Good for You. Good for Me, Good for You.

Parents report that this simple technique gives them a warm, furry feeling of not caring about their teens at all. It makes them feel better instantly.

Power visualization

Nothing causes more stress than living with teens. Scientists have proven that you can reduce stress with visualization, the art of mentally picturing your problem, then picturing how you want things to be.

Example: 17-year-old Chuck says he and 6 friends are going to drive 1500 miles to a rap music concert, in an open pick-up truck, in the middle of January. Father experiences crushing headache, bile rising to his throat, constricted breathing and an overwhelming sense of panic.

Father goes to his room, shuts his eyes and pictures the problem. In his mind's eye, Father reduces Chuck to a tiny mosquito, which he flicks away with his pinkie finger. Father has added 6 months to his life expectancy.

A short-cut to this method, the One-Minute Visualization, is described on page 77.

Pendulum Power and Parent Power

New Age practitioners draw shamelessly from ancient wisdom, so why shouldn't you? Try pendulumism, the art of handling a pendulum so that it reveals the energy fluctuations in any object—including your teen.

> **Example:** Your family is enjoying a pleasant dinner until someone asks your 15-year-old daughter to pass the salt. She leaps out of her chair, knocks it over, screams "FIGHT THE POWER!" and stomps from the room. Everyone falls silent and sits wide-eyed and trembling.

When your daughter sits down to dinner, let the pendulum swing behind her back. Immediately you will know whether you will be dining with the Hopeless Monster (pendulum tends to the right), the Reasonable Human Being (pendulum swings to the left), the Tiny Baby (pendulum curls up), etc. If the

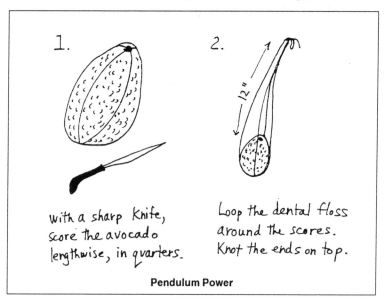

1. With a sharp Knife, score the avocado lengthwise, in quarters.

2. Loop the dental floss around the scores. Knot the ends on top.

Pendulum Power

pendulum is absolutely still, you should employ Non-lingual messaging interpretation (page 56); if it seems actually to rise in the air, try Power Parenting with the underside of the brain (*see below*); if you can't figure out what the pendulum is doing, just say, "Good for you" (page 35). Better yet, go out for dinner and leave her there with a frozen pizza.

The pendulum need not be a fancy store-bought model. Rig up your own with an avocado and a piece of dental floss.

Power Parenting with the underside of the brain

The right brain/left brain theory says that our brains are divided into two hemispheres: the left brain, home of logical thought, and the right brain, home of creativity and intuition. In parents of teenagers there is a third brain segment, the Underside of the Brain.

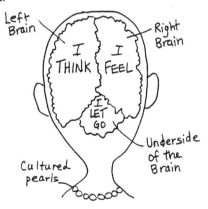

The Parent's Brain

The underside is chaos-controlled and filled with random particles. Left dormant, it just uses up space between your ears. But when it is activated, look out! Primal, powerful, fiendish

Power Parenting solutions are released from the underside of the brain.

> **Example:** 14-year-old Nathan is 5 feet tall and not growing. His friends tower over him, as does the shortest girl in his class. Nathan is apathetic and listless. His grades take a nose dive. He stops watching TV, bathing and, finally, going outdoors.

Father lies down in a darkened room and concentrates on his problem. Then he bounces the problem back and forth between his right brain and his left brain, logic to intuition, faster and faster until particle fission occurs and a brilliant, obvious solution emerges. He experiences this state as "white light," "hot," and "explosive." A week later, he goes on a TV game show and wins a complete home workout rig. Nathan is still 5 feet tall, but his new powerful body brings him respect, admiration and success among the Grade Nines.

> **Example:** Laurie, 15, has a serious heavy metal music addiction. Day and night the sounds of Slayer and Iron Maiden throb through the tiny house. Mother cannot afford the ideal Power Parent solution—building a separate residence for Laurie. She is starting to lose it.

Mother practises Power Parenting from the underside of the brain, described above, and creates "Turn off Metallica–Turn on Mozart," one of our Subliminal Subversion Tapes (see Power Parent Enhancement Products, page 90). Now Mother and Laurie go about their business to the strains of gentle baroque music.

Self-parenting and self-power-parenting

Many people have discovered that their own parents neglected them, and they are turning to self-parenting as a way to get mothered as they should have been in the first place. What a great solution for teens, who always hate their real parents!

> **Example:** Naomi, 14, likes to spend money but refuses to accept jobs babysitting or carrying newspapers because they pay "zero money." She asks Father for a hefty allowance.

Father encourages Naomi to visualize the perfect parent and to turn to that inner parent whenever she needs it. Then he wisely does not contradict Naomi's self-parent. "Talk to the parent within," he tells her, "think of me as the parent without." He goes out dancing.

Chaos Power Parenting

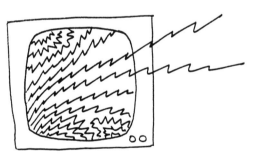

Chaos Power

Chaos theory is the science of patterns of unpredictability. Parents of teenagers, and only parents of teenagers, understand this concept—that rational, safe, knowable facts are nothing but a complex set of both random and organized data.

69

Example: Your 16-year-old daughter is a whiz at calculus, but she thinks pregnancy is something that happens to other people.

Example: Your 15-year-old son is a vegetarian and peace activist who beats the bejesus out of his younger brother once a month.

After years of expensive experiments, eminent chaos theorists have accepted the mysteries of the universe by arriving at the nucleus of Power Parenting: Don't say no, just let go.

Other New Realities

Channelling

Get in touch with James Dean, Buddy Holly or the teen angel of your choice. Let them speak through you, directly to your teen. Fortunately you, as the medium, won't even have to listen to the conversation.

Karmic Parenting

You reap what you sow. Give your teen the kind of Power Parents you wish you had, instead of the repressive, violent, abusive and otherwise "involved" parents you actually did have.

Zen Parenting (Less Is More)

What is the sound of one Power Parent ignoring her teen's choice of associates? Blissful silence.

FROM MARIA'S MAILBAG

Dear Maria:

My daughter dyes her hair jet black every month, even though she has gorgeous natural red hair and the dye gives her severe allergic reactions, such as asthma and open running sores. I just can't stand to see her like this!
— *Broken*, Comox, B.C.

Dear Broken,

Then don't look.

—Maria

Dear Maria:

I was shocked the other day to discover my son and his friends lighting each other's farts. Surely this is not acceptable behaviour for a young man!
— *Chagrined*, Kenora, Ont.

Dear Chagrined:

Are you kidding? Did you ever hear of Robert Bly? Get a grip, Chagrined! Your son is sitting on a gold mine.

—Maria

CHAPTER ELEVEN

Letting Go, Kicking Out & Living It Up

Most teens dream of leaving home. But some teens dream of staying home forever. I have met parents of 22, 25, even 27-year-old teenagers! When the Reasonable Human Being in your teen says "Let's get the heck out of here" and the Tiny Baby drowns it out with a powerful "And give up free room and board?", you need the Power Parenting method, even if you got by without it before.

> **Example:** Candice, 21, has flunked out of two colleges and lost three jobs since graduating high school.
>
> ✓ **The pre-Power Parent sequence:** Mother calls a friend and persuades her to hire Candice. Candice goes to work. Mother collects rent. Candice quits her job. Mother persuades her to get re-hired. Candice quits her job. Mother gets Candice a student loan and admission into a college 2,000 miles away. Candice quits school and comes home. Mother introduces Candice to a nice boy at the plant. Candice falls in love with the nice boy and moves in with him. The

nice boy loses his job. He and Candice and their new baby move back in with Mother.

✓ **The Power Parent sequence:** Mother turns her home into a halfway house for recovering workaholics. Candice and family move out for good.

Example: Richard does nothing but eat, sleep and watch TV.

✓ **The pre-Power Parent sequence:** Father sells the TV. Richard does nothing but eat and sleep. Father removes all food from the suite and takes his meals at Helen's Grill. Richard does nothing but sleep. Father cuts a hole in the roof of Richard's bedroom, as if for a skylight, but never installs the skylight. Richard covers the hole with green garbage bags and does nothing but sleep. Father turns the suite into a tourist attraction, charging visitors $3 ($2 unemployed) to observe a superannuated adolescent in his natural habitat. Richard does nothing but sleep. Father wakes Richard up and offers him a 1964 Oldsmobile and $400 in cash if he will leave. Richard goes back to sleep.

✓ **The Power Parent sequence:** Father gives notice and moves into a bachelor apartment. Richard is removed by the new tenants.

Important note: Do not jump the gun. Employ one of the Power Parenting methods only when you are sure your teen has passed through all six stages of leaving home:

73

The six stages of leaving home

Stage 1—the first time

Stage 2—the second time

Stage 3—the prepenultimate time

Stage 4—the penultimate time

Stage 5—the ultimate time

Stage 6—the return

Your teen has permanently left home when:

✓ All LPs, audiotapes and CDs are gone from your home except Handel's *Water Music* and the soundtrack from *West Side Story*.

✓ A box of potato chips lasts longer than 2 hours.

✓ Your hot water bill is so low you think there must be a terrible mistake.

✓ All high school annuals and moldy prom corsages are gone from your teen's room.

✓ You find out your teen is listed with Directory Assistance.

✓ Your dining room furniture has disappeared.

✓ Your teen calls to invite you to lunch and please bring your chequebook.

CHAPTER TWELVE

The One–Minute Mother: *Power parenting in the fast lane*

One-Minute Motherhood is based on two assumptions:

- ✓ No teenager can listen to her parent for more than 1 minute;

- ✓ A mother should be able to assume absolute power over her teen in 1 minute or less per day.

Anyone—yes, anyone, even a father—can become a One-Minute Mother. With practice, you can replace 24 hours of desperate anxiety with 60 seconds of a simple, fun, effective exercise.

The One-Minute Affirmation

Don't say no. The Power Parent knows it is always easier to say yes, especially these days when positivity has become a sort of religion.

> **Examples:**
> TEEN: My period is late.
> MOTHER: I'm so glad you aren't sexually repressed.

> TEEN: I'm selling your washing machine and buying a dirt bike.
> MOTHER: You are so unselfish! Any other boy would want to have both.

 ## The One-Minute Priorization

Take 60 seconds a day to priorize. Remind yourself of what really matters.

> **Example:** Your son has been caught smoking dope in a suburban shopping mall. His grades are slipping, he has let his hair grow down to his nose and a youth gang has been coming around asking for him.

What really matters:

✓ You just won $10 in the lottery.

✓ The world has not yet been destroyed by nuclear war.

> **Example:** Your daughter spent all her birthday money on a tape recorder, which she uses to record compromising conversations between her brother and his girlfriend. Then she blackmails them.

76

What really matters:

✓ You will not have to replace your car for at least another year.

✓ The weather is improving.

 ## The One-Minute Visualization

Your imagination can be your best friend when it comes to your teen. Creative visualization works for winning athletes and it works for winning Power Parents.

> **Example:** Picture your teen coming home from a day of honours classes and virtuous extracurriculars. She kisses your cheek and asks you for your opinion on important current events. After helping you prepare dinner, she eats enthusiastically but not sloppily. She then puts on a gorgeous outfit that she bought at a thrift store, and goes out with her boyfriend, who is her age but mature, smart and quite wealthy. She comes home before curfew with no hickeys on her neck.

The impressionable Power Parent is soothed and healed by this vision, and the more cynical Power Parent is so nauseated by it that she starts thinking her real-life teen ain't so bad after all.

 ## The One-Minute Euphemism

You can talk yourself out of a teen-induced anxiety attack by taking 60 seconds to re-word the problem. After all, it is easier to manipulate yourself than to manipulate your teen. Don't be afraid to appropriate the language of psychologists, New Age therapists and common liars.

Examples:

WRONG: Brent has spoken only 2 syllables in 3 years.

RIGHT: Brent has found his own quiet path to inner psycho-spiritual awareness.

WRONG: Susan has a police record longer than your arm.

RIGHT: Susan is committed to personal freedom.

WRONG: Adam wets the bed.

RIGHT: Adam is so in touch with the small child within himself.

WRONG: Tina is anorexic.

RIGHT: Tina has designed a successful fitness program.

WRONG: My teenagers are out of control.

RIGHT: I have liberated my family from its confining knots.

 The One-Minute Duck-Backing

Just let go. Take as your role model the humble duck, which simply lets water, mud and sewage slide off its back.

> **Example:** Your son has spent 1½ hours locked in the bathroom, and has flushed the toilet six times.

> **Example:** Your daughter has fallen deeply in love with a 30-year-old married man, who has promised to wait until she is 14 to have sex with her.

The Power Parent would not waste more than 1 minute on either of these events. Lie down, shut your eyes and breathe slowly and deeply for 60 seconds, picturing yourself on an

Alaskan cruise. Or just go to the kitchen and make yourself a large hot fudge sundae.

Let it slide off, let it all slide off. You have nothing to lose but your own panic.

 ## The One-Minute Guilt Trip

When all else fails, take back your power with this time-tested last-ditch method. It takes only 60 seconds a day to nail yourself to the cross.

> **Example:** Sure, honey, you take the car. The buses don't run after midnight but not many muggers will be out in the pouring rain, and anyway I've got to start getting used to this prosthesis.

> **Example:** Of course I can spare $20! You know, just the other day I heard that it costs $110,000 to raise a child to maturity—not including a university education.

FROM MARIA'S MAILBAG

Dear Maria:

Why would a bright, attractive 14-year-old girl spend an entire summer in a windowless basement room, watching TV and eating taco chips?

— *Distressed*, Moncton, N.B.

Dear Distressed:

Why would you notice, when you're at the beach all day with your pals?

— *Maria*

Dear Maria:

My wife and I went out of town last weekend. When we came home, the neighbours told us that our 17-year-old son had spent the entire time entertaining party-animal friends, with the help of our food, our liquor, our CDs, and our bed. We need a new approach.

— *Indignant*, Hay River, N.W.T.

Dear Indignant:

Wrong! You need new neighbours.

— *Maria*

PART THREE

Getting from where you are to where you wanted to be in the first place

CHAPTER THIRTEEN

The Power Parenting Check-In

The road to Power Parenthood can be a rocky one. Some parents adapt to the practice of creative neglect as if they were born to it, flinging their guilt to the winds almost immediately. Others, the ones I call Process Freaks, need frequent concrete demonstrations of their progress and reassurance that they are not being irresponsible. For them, there is the Power Parenting Check-In.

Designed to help you quantify your pain, the Check-In will remind you that others have it even worse than you do. It will help you spot your own incremental gains and, in the last throes of pre-Power Parenting, it will even help remind you of simple facts, such as your own name.

Copy the questionnaire and fill it out once a week. Each time you do it, notice how you are changing—moving, as you will, through debilitating guilt and the desire for vengeance, to manic self-loathing and self-mockery, to teen-mockery and harsh bouts of uncontrollable laughter, to resignation and then acceptance. When you start forgetting to fill it out, or it begins to seem like just too much hassle, you will know that you are well on your way to Power Parenthood.

FOR THE LAST SEVEN DAYS:

My name has been: _____

My teen's name has been: _____

My age: _____ Age of my teen: _____

Number of disagreements between me and my teen: _____

   % minor arguments (garbage not taken out, 30-min. showers): _____

   % major arguments (live rats in bedroom, expulsion from school): _____

   % physical confrontations without permanent injuries: _____

   % physical confrontations with permanent injuries (specify): _____

   _____

   _____

   % other (specify:): _____

   _____

   _____

Number of meals my teen ate at home: _____

Number of meals remaining (21 minus the above answer): _____

   % eaten in a good home (estimate): _____

   % eaten in a good restaurant (estimate): _____

   % eaten in a bad home (estimate): _____

   % eaten in a bad restaurant (estimate): _____

   % consisting of cheezies, chips, pop, etc. (estimate): _____

   % skipped altogether (estimate): _____

Amount of household food my teen consumed between meals: _____

_____

Amount of household food my teen's friends consumed between meals:

_____

Number of hours my teen spent in the bathroom: _____

Number of hours I spent in the bathroom: _____

Number of dollars my teen cadged off me: _____

Number of times the school counsellor phoned to
   say s/he was "concerned": _____

Number of times the school counsellor phoned to
   say s/he was "extremely concerned": _____

Number of times my teen referred to
   the school counsellor as a "dick-head": _____

Number of times my teen changed hair style: _____

Number of times my teen changed hair colour: _____

Number of new items of clothing my teen was seen wearing: _____

   % purchased (estimate): _____

   % borrowed (estimate): _____

   % traded for something less valuable (estimate): _____

   % traded for something more valuable (estimate): _____

   % stolen from me (estimate): _____

   % stolen from others (estimate): _____

Number of words spoken to me by my teen: _____

   % pleasant: _____

   % insufferably rude: _____

   % inaudible: _____

Number of times my teen spent more than 1 hour lying on
   the bed listening to a rock'n'roll song over and over: _____

Number of hours my teen spent looking in the mirror: _____

Number of hours my teen spent perfecting a new signature: _____

Number of hours my teen spent on the telephone: _____

   % gossip and backbiting (estimate): _____

   % schoolwork (estimate): _____

   % phone sex (estimate): _____

Number of times my teen said "OK OK, don't have a cow,

    I'm hanging up": _____

Number of times my teen found fault with my hair style: _____

Number of times my teen found fault with my clothing: _____

Number of times my teen found fault with my political beliefs: _____

Number of times my teen found fault with my breath: _____

Number of times my teen found fault with something else

    I can't help (specify): _____

    _____

    _____

Number of mildew-covered dishes found in my teen's room: _____

Number of mildew-covered socks found in my teen's room: _____

Number of times my teen was obviously bored: _____

Number of times my teen was obviously drugged: _____

Number of times my teen was obviously in trouble with the police: _____

Number of hours I spent in tears because of my teen: _____

Number of hours of sleep I lost because of my teen: _____

Number of excuses I made for my teen's unacceptable behaviour: _____

Number of lies I told friends and family about

    how well my teen is doing: _____

Number of times I read my teen's diary, desperate

    to know what the heck was going on with him/her: _____

Amount of prescription drugs I had to

    consume to cope with my teen: _____

Amount of non-prescription drugs I had to

    consume to cope with my teen: _____

Number of times my teen ran away: _____

Number of times I ran away: _____

CHAPTER FOURTEEN

The Power Parenting Bookshelf

Power Parenting is one great idea that takes many forms. As you become more proficient at the method, you may feel the need for further reassurance or new inspirations, tailored to your own individual lifestyle. Here are a few of my favourite books:

Five Minutes a Day for a Greener Parent-Teen Relationship
Bobbi Shrimp
Combining ecography and psychography, Shrimp offers 100 quick-fix plans to healthier home dynamics. Five-minute sessions include smudging (ritual burning of bits of your teen's hair), daydreamwork (similar to Creative Visualization), aromatherapy (learning to enjoy the odour of your teen's running shoes).

One Foot In Front of the Other
Tara Flaubert
A book of meditations and affirmations for the emerging Power Parent—one thought for each day of the year. March 8 entry: "Happy International Women's Day! The ILGWU did not gain power by trying to understand the garment

moguls, so must you take your own power without trying to understand your teens."

Grief Relief
Richard Miyake, M.D.
The author proposes that the agony of parenting teens stems from your sadness over the loss of your tiny, dependent, manipulable babies. Though grieving is very fashionable these days, I wouldn't recommend this text except for its list of suggested grief-soothers: extended partying, profligate consumption of comfort foods, and multi-directional whining.

Teen Havens
Roberta Perroni
Here are scores of useful and well-illustrated tips on how to create a separate dwelling space for adolescents, whether you live in a sprawling mansion or a ghetto apartment. Includes complete instructions on turning unused crawl spaces into teen alcoves, winterizing ordinary nylon pup tents and sneaking around the building code to renovate the garage.

The Tao of Power Parenting
rNBOP.XING.LO
The teen . . . the parent . . . the wind . . . the ocean . . . the car parts rusting in the back yard . . . all are one. You and your teen are infinite in space and time. You can't own your teen, your teen can't own you. When you don't push, your teen can't push back. And so on.

Shop for Transformation
Pépé Juarez de Catarina
Looking for a way to beat those teen-parenting doldrums? This comprehensive guide to escape-shopping covers every-

thing from the well-planned weekend West Edmonton Mall excursion, to the emergency mental-health impulse-buying binge in your own neighbourhood. Tours involve no unrecyclable plastic bags and no products tested on animals with cute faces.

The Goodness! Book of Teen Records
Smart Alec Goodness
Open this little booklet to any page for the most shocking and embarrassing true teen tales the authors could assemble— much worse than anything your teen will do. Examples: the mother who bought her 16-year-old son goods and services worth $46,577 to get him to go live with his father, the 17-year-old who invoked the Freedom of Information Act to get access to her mother's anguish-filled diaries, etc.

CHAPTER FIFTEEN

Power Parenting Enhancement Products

One of the keys to becoming a true Power Parent is treating yourself extremely well and quite often. Look for these effective and comforting products in your neighbourhood therapy boutique today.

Let It All Go Stereo Radio Headphones

This deluxe set, made of flexible state-of-the-art foam-padded plastic, allows you to block out all unwanted noise, such as the sound of your teens fighting with each other or telling you their vocational plans for the future. Radio included, which electronically scans for and scrambles all stations catering to teenagers.

Power Parenting Cheat Sheet

It is easy to forget the "Good for you" rule when your teen is standing in front of you blaming you for your haircut, her haircut, the bus

90

schedule and world hunger. Slip the Cheat Sheet's comfortable elastic band around your arm, slide the vinyl-covered, tastefully lettered list of keywords into your sleeve, and you will never again be caught without the proper Power Parent response.

Power Parenting Audio Prompt

Designed for those situations where the Power Parenting Cheat Sheet is inconvenient (i.e. when you are at the beach or sound asleep), this tiny, ingenious device fits snugly around your ear. It is programmed to respond to your teen's voice with the whispered words, "Say 'Good for you'."

Flux Ointment

This potent, soothing emollient was formulated for the transition periods of Power Parenthood. In the weeks when you are saying "Good for you" through clenched teeth because you don't quite believe it yet, Flux Ointment provides temporary relief from hemorrhoids. Later in your learning period, when you may occasionally find yourself swallowing your pride, Flux will ease the way.

Single-Malt Double-Shot
Triple-Strength Whiskey Samplers

The quickies in this compact case, standing only 3" high, slide easily under any bed, even a postmodern futon. The perfect companions to moments of crisis, they are teen-proofed with digitized locks which can be opened only by punching in your Parent Identity Code.

Power Parenting Subliminal Subversion Tapes

Train your teen's brain the E-Z way with these motivational tapes, which speak to your teen's subconscious mind. After all, there's no point in talking to their conscious minds. Processed with ultra-sophisticated equipment, the tapes play simultaneously with rock audio tapes, CDs, and any radio station. 35,000 subliminal messages per hour are embedded in teens' favourite music—but they are aware of no aural interference! Titles include: *I Want to Clean My Room, I'm Going to Get a Job, I Want to Get My Hair Cut, I Want to Let My Hair Grow, I Can't Wait to Visit Grammi and Gramps, I'm Never Going to See That Boy Again, Let Me at That Pile of Dirty Dishes, Turn off Metallica–Turn on Mozart.*

The Power Parenting Training Video

Seeing is believing! The producers have created dramatic re-enactments of hair-raising true-life problems and Power Parenting solutions in action: 14-year-old Patricia, who became a train-hopping rock band groupie; 17-year-old Ichabod, who infected his parents' business equipment with twenty different insidious computer viruses; Shannon, who at age 15 graduated from stealing cars to stealing airplanes. 82 minutes, Beta only (Power Parenting has been around a long, long time).

Index